The
Romantic
English
Garden

The
Romantic
English
Garden

Authorized Purveyors

VICTORIA'S SECRET

Nº 10 MARGARET STREET · LONDON W1

Contents

And all without were walkes and alleys dight

With divers trees enrang'd in even rankes;

And here and there were pleasant arbours pight,

And shadie seats, and sundry flow'ring bankes,

To sit and rest the walkers wearie shanks:

And therein thousand payres of lovers walkt,

Praysing their god, and yeelding him great thankes.

EDMUND SPENSER, ?1552–99

The Romantic Garden

Every garden can be said to represent the search for a personal paradise. Little wonder, then, that in the great gardens of both past and present there is a strong sense of the romantic. Some reveal themselves willingly to the visitor; others are slower to unfold their charms. Some are romantic, by virtue of their design and planting style or perhaps their

ROSE *Love*

The rose has been associated with love, and with marriage, for centuries. A bouquet of red roses still signifies 'I love you'. Rose petals were strewn on the ground before the bride and bridegroom and scattered on their heads.

situation; others have earned the quality of romance because of the lives of those who made them and loved them. The earliest gardens of which we have any knowledge were made in desert lands, where parching sun contrasted with the cool shade of trees, and where dry soil was nourished by the precious water captured in rills and fountains and streams. To this day, our gardens remain a spiritual oasis, a haven from the stresses that surround us in everyday life. The ideal garden is traditionally that of Eden, a natural garden of beautiful plants and cooling waters; a garden very like the Persian concept of paradise. The word paradise, indeed, derives from the Persian word for a garden.

There is, of course, a style – in the visual arts, in literature, – known as Romantic. An appreciation of the beauty of nature unadorned, untamed was one of its manifestations. Once much of the European landscape had been subdued to man's needs, the wildness of what remained untouched seemed to have an emotive appeal. People of means, endowed with both leisure and sensibility, came to appreciate the beauty and grandeur of mountains and streams, moorlands and ancient forests.

The first English gardens which began to express this new reverence for nature were of the kind now called landscape gardens. Their most famous advocate was 'Capability' Brown. These must have seemed striking at first, in contrast to the rough fields and copses around them. These contoured grounds, with their lakes, artfully disposed clumps of trees, and smooth grass that lopped the very foot of the grand houses they embraced, the serenely classical face of the romantic vision of the eighteenth-century.

Another kind of Eden followed, in which exotic plants from distant lands were tried and found to be beautiful. One of the most notable creators was Repton, who gave great impetus to the development of the exotically romantic garden. After him, no single school of garden design was dominant in England, and the characteristic impulses of romanticism, the emphasis on feeling over reason, emotion over intellect, were given free rein in a host of intensely personal gardens.

The Romance of the past is always a potent force: the very formal gardens of medieval and Tudor times, the knot gardens of Elizabethan England or the geometric herb gardens of ancient monasteries are now consciously echoed in gardens of the present.

The most enduring image of the garden in England for the past century, however, has been the cottage garden. As interpreted by innumerable skilled hands, often those of dedicated amateurs, the cottage garden is a wholly romanticized vision of the patchwork of little plots cultivated by cottage-dwellers, the labourers of the past. They had no leisure in which to grow unproductive flowers; most, if not all, of their modest acreage was made to yield produce to feed their children. Independent means were needed to enjoy the luxury of bright flower borders beneath espaliered apple trees, of clipped box hedges around a tangle of old-fashioned flowers, of fragrant pinks with names like an echo from the past – Sops in Wine, Painted Lady, Nutmeg Clove – spilling over the ragged paving of cottage paths.

In these pages, then, you will find formal gardens, cottage gardens, grand gardens and smaller, intensely personal gardens.

Even a garden without a house – such as Stourhead – can seem romantic, but most gardens belong to and with a house, which may add its own note of romance whether a moated castle, a medieval timbered hall, a sober stone mansion, a Palladian villa: each carries a weight of associations. A successful garden is in harmony with the house, reinforcing its personality. It is not really a question of precise historical accuracy – a richly planted garden such as

Sissinghurst would be a very different place if the only plants growing there were those known at the time the castle was built, in Tudor and Elizabethan times – but of the enduring spirit of the place.

Experiencing a garden, you are briefly a visitor in paradise. For gardens appeal to all the senses. The best time to visit a garden, if you can, is in the early morning or late afternoon, when the sun is low and the light less stark than at midday. Then the lengthening shadows of evening, or the crispness of morning, add another quality to the patterns of flower and foliage, of light and dark, of texture and fragrance, that compose the garden scene. Then, too, the power of association seems to work more strongly where wafts of fragrance arouse nostalgic evocations of days gone by; long shadows across a smooth lawn conjure up images of afternoon tea beneath the cedar's spreading branches, served by a curtseying maidservant or a suave butler to ladies in long dresses and bonnets.

HONEYSUCKLE

Sweetness of Disposition

The message of the honeysuckle
is a simple one; the exquisite fragrance
of the flower stands for the sweet nature of
the one who gives it. If the knot that tied
the posy was to the left, the flowers spoke
of the sender; if to the right, of the recipient.

The timeless elements in all gardens are light and shade, earth, stone and water, foliage and flowers. They combine to give us movement – the ripple of water, the flicker of light through leaves – and sound, colour and fragrance. Fragrance, indeed, is another reason for visiting gardens in the evening; for many plants are more powerfully scented at dusk and some only then. What is more, evening fragrance is free-floating; the very air is filled with clouds of perfume. Sometimes a particular memory is called to mind in a flash: sometimes, just a diffuse and poignant nostalgia. The sense of romance, too, is in part a kind of nostalgia for a never-experienced perfection, in which the air is neither too cool nor too hot, and always smells sweet.

The very names of the fragrant flowers that abound in many English gardens testify to their long-time popularity: honeysuckle and sweet rocket, sweet William and sweet pea and evening primrose, lad's love and sweet brier. Botanical names are essential for accuracy but cherry pie sounds more appealing than *Heliotropium*, and wintersweet than *Chimonanthus praecox*.

There is romance, too, in the sounds of the garden: the sudden muting of the insistent twentieth century roar as you pass through high hedges into the enclosures within; the sweep of the wind through branches; emphasizing still further the sense of seclusion from the rigours of the outside world; the patter of leaves in the breeze; the fall of water in fountains and streams; the songs of birds. No wonder that early English settlers, homesick for familiar things, called the American birds by English names – the robin is the best known – and the plants by the name of the English plant they most resembled. Witch hazel was a reminder of the unrelated common hazel that bears its edible nuts in English nut walks and coppices, and the

My garden all is overblown with roses,

My spirit all is overblown with rhyme,

As like a drunken honeybee I waver

From house to garden and again to house

And, undetermined which delight to favour

On verse and rose alternately carouse.

VITA SACKVILLE-WEST *Sonnet*

nodding blue flowers of Virginian cowslip, though different in colour, of the fragrant yellow bells of the cowslip of English meadows.

Then there are incidents in the garden which underline the sense of romance. A flowery arbour, decked with roses and honeysuckle, calls to mind the dalliance of Henry II of England and Rosamund; a garden sheltered behind enclosing walls holds echoes of Frances Hodgson Burnett's classic for children, *The Secret Garden*, where fragrant roses succeed the tiny bulbs of spring, piercing through grass that no foot has trod for years.

If the secret garden, the fragrant arbour, are inward looking, garden vistas lead the eye onward, and often outward, beyond the garden boundaries to the landscape beyond. English gardens abound in vistas, where the visitor is enticed towards a beautiful view, or towards a focal point by the masterly placing of the garden's components.

The English spirit is essentially poetic and romantic, seeking to create the ideal blend of both nature and art. England has, of course, her great poets but the island race has produced more than its share of those who express their love of beauty in the creation of a garden.

Evocation of the Past

BARNSLEY HOUSE · GLOUCESTERSHIRE

The beautiful garden that surrounds the seven-teenth-century manor house of honey-coloured Cotswold stone is almost a compendium of garden styles, a living history book. In one small compass you can pass from an Elizabethan knot garden to a pretty twentieth-century flower border, from an

eighteenth-century temple to a romantic wilderness of graceful trees set in meadow grass.

In this essentially peaceful garden, there is a sense of changing moods, where simplicity contrasts with elements of surprise. The miniature knot garden near the house, made of clipped germander, lavender and box in a frame of rosemary, is composed of two intricate patterns inspired by the formal designs of the past, as is the patterned herb garden set in decorative paving.

Yet there is an unconventional air, too. At right angles to the house is a paved walk flanked by pairs of sentinel Irish yews. No longer is the path made for treading upon, however, for it is filled with pink, rose and white rock roses, growing between the flagstones.

At one end of the main vista is the Tuscan temple, standing in a paved garden, its image reflected in the still surface of a pool rimmed with water lilies.

The most striking feature of the garden, in its brief season, is the laburnum arbour forming a vista of living sunlight. White variegated hostas beneath with the mauve globes of *Allium affatunense* (best of the ornamental aliums with its tall stems and bold heads), and golden lemon balm appear like patches of fallen sun beneath the canopy.

The scent of flowers permeates the house throughout the seasons. The delectably perfumed shrubs of winter are grouped close by so their sweetness can be inhaled without braving inclement weather. In summer, pots of lemon verbena and fragrant-leaved geraniums stand on the terraces, inviting the liberating touch of the passer-by.

The flower borders are inspired by great artist-gardeners of the past, names like Gertrude Jekyll or Nancy Lancaster whose descriptions of old roses are so romantic, so that a deep reverence for the past and a sense of the romance of history is apparent in every corner of this varied, tranquil, and very personal garden.

A Sense of Mystery

SCOTNEY CASTLE · KENT

Scotney stands in a uniquely dramatic and romantic setting, a ruined fourteenth-century castle surrounded by a lake and bounded by woodland gardens. It is a place of enchantment where the sunlight glints off still waters. Yet Scotney at dusk on a rainy autumn day is both melancholy and mysterious; it might be the very moated grange from which Tennyson's unhappy Mariana gazed out, weeping.

The castle in its watery hollow, though stoutly constructed, was damp and cold. In the mid-ninetenth century, the Hussey family (whose ancestors first acquired Scotney in 1778) built a comfortable country house on high ground nearby. Around the old castle and timbered, fortified manor house, carefully reduced to a picturesque ruin, the family set out to create a deliberately romantic garden.

They planted trees and shrubs in abundance rhododendrons and fragrant azaleas, huge kalmias or calico bushes, magnolias and Japanese maples are spread beneath the great beeches, oaks and limes of

Meadows trim with daisies pied,
Shallow brooks and rivers wide.
Towers, and battlements it sees
Bosom'd high in tufted trees
Where perhaps some beauty lies
The cynosure of neighbouring eyes.

MILTON: L'Allegro

an English woodland and contrast with the dramatic accents of American conifers.

Emerging by cool shaded walks from this beautifully composed woodland, brilliant with rhododendron blooms in spring and blazing foliage in autumn, one encounters the castle ruins, its ancient walls decked in old fragrant roses. Here are 'Shakespeare's Musk' and 'Rambling Rector', their great swags of creamy blossoms, a hundred blooms in each, filling the air with heady perfume. Blush and pink rambling roses mingle with white wisteria, while at their feet, aromatic herbs add their scent in a harmony of sweet fragrance and soft colours that is enriched by deeper tones of crimson and purple from the luscious full-petalled peonies.

By the waterside, hostas and huge gunneras, their bristly stems rasping in the breeze, grow into a lush jungle of foliage mirrored in the lake. In autumn the royal fern's golden fronds echo the bright livery of the woodland flowers.

Scotney is evocative at all seasons: in late spring when the azaleas and calico bushes are in flower, at midsummer when fragrant roses deck the old castle walls, in high summer amid the night-scented tobacco flowers. But perhaps the sense of romance is most strongly felt in autumn, when the leaves are falling, the deep waters of the moat are still and dark, and shadows fall about the tower and the deserted walls and time seems to stand still.

A Garden of Dreams

HADDON HALL · DERBYSHIRE

I n 1697 Haddon Hall was described by a visitor as 'a good old house built of stone on a hill, and behind it is a fine grove of high trees, and good gardens'. Haddon Hall was originally the seat of the Vernon family, who lived here for four hundred years. In the sixteenth century the heiress Dorothy Vernon eloped with her lover, Sir John Manners, during her sister's wedding. The scandal may be imagined; but the family relented and allowed the runaways to marry, and thus the Manners family came to own Haddon in 1567. Later there came to them first

an earldom and in due course a dukedom.

The house seems to have drifted through the years. Built in the fifteenth century, medieval houses were just emerging from the defensiveness of the castle but had yet to relax into the expansive country mansions of more settled times. The terraces and balustrades that Dorothy knew are still there; the worn stone threshold over which, together with generations of Vernons and Manners, she would have passed from house to tranquil garden; the gate through which she ran away and the steps down which she made her way to the packbridge over the river Wye to meet her lover. But the planting is new; for in 1701 the house was virtually shut down and left to slumber for over two hundred years. By the end of the eighteenth century, it had already acquired a sense of mystery and romance as the neglected topiary grew into tall yews shading the terraces, and the house stood shuttered and mute.

In 1912 the family began the work of restoration, a task which was to take a quarter of a century. The overgrown yews, beyond redemption, were felled and replacements now re-create the original

atmosphere of the seventeenth-century garden. Emerging from the house to the broad upper terrace, one sees the garden spread below in its seven descending tiers. The noble balustrade along the edge of the terrace leads down a flight of steps, garlanded in rambler roses, to the fountain garden with its square pool which in turn drops to the garden's lower levels, overlooked by the windows of the Long Gallery.

In keeping with this place of dreams, the planting is overwhelmingly of roses. Tall rambler roses, mingled with clematis, deck the massive buttresses over three hundred years old and worn with time.

Between them, peonies and buddleias soften the severity of the stone work. Perhaps the ninth Duke had in mind, as he re-created the garden and thought of his romantic ancestor, the lines of Matthew Arnold:

> Strew on her roses, roses,
> And never a spray of yew.

The fine grove of trees that graced the view from the Hall is still there, and beyond the river Wye that flows beneath the castle walls lies the landscape of the Peak District, one of the most green and beautiful of England's heartlands.

Timeless Tapestry

SISSINGHURST · KENT

The garden at Sissinghurst, more than any other in the land, is quintessentially English. This has much to do with the people who made it. When Harold Nicolson and his wife Vita Sackville-West first saw Sissinghurst in 1930 it was derelict, the old buildings abandoned in a tangle of weeds and the debris of centuries of careless occupation. But Vita especially was drawn to the place; she had a powerful sense of ancestry, and Sissinghurst had once belonged to her aristocratic forebears.

During the next two to three years, a new and

complex design was laid down, including the clipped yew hedges that seem to have been there as long as the buildings themselves. All that remains of the original moated manor house is the Tudor entrance, the Elizabethan tower and priest's house, and part of the Elizabethan three-sided mansion. Each stands separate from the others, blended now into the firm geometric structure of the garden.

It is a garden of long formal vistas, of secret and private enclosures, full of mystery and surprise; a garden wholly English in character, in tune with the landscape and planted with romantic profusion. Harold Nicolson's contribution lay in the design, the use of the elements of water, trees, hedges and lawns. Vita's was the hand that created the purple

borders, the white garden, the rose garden; she it was who set scented ramblers to clamber through the gnarled fruit trees in the old orchard.

The rose, more than any other plant, epitomizes Sissinghurst. Vita did not care for modern, scentless and soulless roses; she loved the old shrub roses. Their associations with a wonderfully storied past appealed as much as their richness or delicacy of colour, their generous abundance, and their fragrance. It is symbolic that the only garden plant found surviving at Sissinghurst in 1930 was a rose, the Moorish rose. It still grows among the apple trees of Sissinghurst, its branches of mint-green foliage sporting plump, full-petalled blooms of mulberry velvet. As well as roses, old cottage garden plants

abound at Sissinghurst: auriculas and double prim-roses, pinks and pansies. Vita used these old favou-rites, and many of her beloved fragrant plants, to make *pot pourri* from old eighteenth-century recipes.

The White Garden has an ethereal magic all its own. In beds edged with clipped box, white flowers and grey foliage mingle in abundance: lilies and roses and tobacco flowers for fragrance, white peonies and silver cotton lavenders, grey lad's love and the grace-ful weeping silver pear. The white garden is Vita's epitaph. She died in June 1962, and on the service sheet at her funeral were these lines from her poem *The Land:*

> 'She walks among the loveliness she made,
> Between the apple blossom and the water –
> She walks among the patterned pied brocade,
> Each flower her son and every tree her daughter.'

Grand Design

STOURHEAD · WILTSHIRE

A degree of make believe is ever-present in the eighteenth-century English garden; the creation of a mood, the recreation of a landscape from abroad embraced by the English countryside. The creator of Stourhead, Henrey Hoare, must have been a man of outstanding foresight and taste. But to envisage these gardens, to imagine the valley filled with water, the bare downs clothed with woods, the newly created landscape set with temples and grottoes calls for an imaginative and inventive genius.

For in 1740, the romantic, natural garden was as yet unthought of. By damming up two valleys, a

vast lake was created, its banks planted with fir and beech. A gentle slope leads down to the lakeside; the view from this point must surely be one of the most beautiful man-made perspectives in the world. 'The eye is led away over the water . . . to a succession of views and vistas, paler and more misty as they recede. These give the impression of going on, like a dream, for ever.'

Continuing around the lake, the grotto comes into view, still retaining, 'something of the mysteri-

ous and romantic atmosphere that it must have had when Pope's celebrated grotto at Twickenham inspired it.' Steep steps lead down, between moss-covered rocks, to the subterranean cavern below, lit dramatically by an overhead opening. In an alcove of shells and rusticated stone, a sculptured nymph reclines on a chilly couch, over which water from a hidden spring perpetually flows.

Around the end of the lake lies a rustic cottage with a inviting seat. From this romantic vantage

point, the lake can be admired in all its limpid beauty, its tree-clad banks, and in the distance another small classical temple, dedicated to Flora, goddess of flowers. Urns of time-worn stone are set in green swathes and backed by banks of deep pink rhododendrons in spring. In early March the reflections of a hundred tiny daffodils are reflected in the lake against the parchment tint of last year's rushes and the warm maroon-red of the Dogwood. Lawns are enlivened by extensive carpets of Lenten lilies and later by bluebells which flower with the scented yellow azaleas, their fragrance wafting on the evening air. In autumn, banks overspread by beeches and covered by the russet of their fallen leaves are reflected in the still waters of the lake, creating a mirror-image of autumnal colours. Standing near the Weeping Larch on the south shore, the winter sun can be seen lighting up the orange-twigged willows on one of the islands while the woodland beyond lies in deep shadow. A classical paradise indeed.

A Vision of Spring

And time remembered is grief
    forgotten,

And frosts are slain and flowers
    begotten,

And in green underwood and cover

Blossom by blossom the spring begins.

SWINBURNE *Atalanta in Calydon*

The Ancient Garden

For almost as long as mankind has lived on this earth, a garden has represented Paradise, a place of beauty and refuge, an ordered place. Romance, for our ancestors, lay not in the wild beauty of mountains and rivers, forest and glen, but in trim plots, clipped evergreens and smooth, ruler-straight paths. Plants were valued above all for their utility: the neat geometric beds would be filled with medicinal plants, with aromatic herbs, with dye plants and with fragrant flowers for the bees.

If any flower was planted for ornament alone, it would most likely be the double, full-petalled variant that someone with an observant eye had spotted in the hedgerow or meadow: double primroses and meadow cranesbill, double celandine and double lady's smock.

What was Paradise? but a garden, full of pleasure,
and nothing there but delights.

WILLIAM LAWSON, 1617

The earliest references to gardens are found in the fourteenth-century *Canterbury Tales*, by the poet Geoffrey Chaucer. By Elizabethan times, we know that clove pinks and columbines, flag iris and lilies were grown with such aromatic herbs as rosemary and lavender, sage and cotton lavender: imports from Mediterranean lands. It is difficult for us, now, to appreciate the enormous importance of aromatic and sweet-smelling plants in those days, when sanitation was primitive as is evident from these lines by a sixteenth century writer:

> My gardens sweet, enclosed with walles strong,
> Embanked with benches to sit and take my rest
> The Knots so enknotted, it cannot be exprest,
> With arbours and alleys so pleasant and so dulce
> The pestilent airs with flavours to repulse.

Many old plants were used in the preparation of med-

In the sixteenth century, the making of gardens became a pleasurable pursuit and arbours, cloaked in fragrant climbers were a popular feature. From them, the delights of a colourful and scent-filled garden could be enjoyed in shaded comfort.

icine (or, as it was then called, physick) or of fragrant waters: Apothecary's Rose; common sage; medicinal rhubarb, and many others.

In Tudor times topiary was already popular (it was originally a Roman fashion) as well as the simple flowers that are now thought of as cottage garden plants. These were set in plain square or rectangular beds, or in more elaborate designs, surrounded by a wall or fence, or by pleached hornbeam or yew. The maze, known already in Henry II's time (he wooed Fair Rosamond in a secret bower at the heart of a maze, where she was fatally discovered by Queen Eleanor) was still popular in Elizabethan times.

During the Jacobean period that followed the formal style was still fashionable. Walled enclosures featured arched trellises, parterres of flowers, arbours and square fish ponds. Again, most of the actual gardens of that period have gone; surviving from around 1650 is the topiary garden at Packwood House, Warwickshire, where simple yew shapes are said to represent the Sermon on the Mount. The true legacy of the period is the plants that were introduced from overseas: the mulberry and apricot, the tulip tree and the cabbage rose.

In 1685 William and Mary came to the throne of England, and brought with them the influence of the Dutch style, for William of Orange was a Dutch-man. In Holland, the grandeur of French formal gardens had been tempered by the Dutch genius for domesticity; and this proved to be a style well suited to the English temperament. The rigid patterns of canals in flat terrain were enlivened by orangeries and pavilions, trees in tubs, clipped hedges, statuary and topiary. It was a style that could be adapted both to a great house and to a more modest dwelling. The gardens at Henry VIII's Hampton Court owe their present form to William and Mary.

A less grand survivor from those days is the garden at Westbury Court, Gloucestershire, made between 1696 and 1705. A long canal with a tall pavilion on a four-pillared loggia at one end and a T-crossing canal is set in clipped yew hedges; a small formal parterre has been recreated in the original design, and the old varieties of orchard fruits and of flowers are once again grown on the boundary walls.

Like Westbury, Melbourne Hall in Derbyshire survived due to neglect, so that it was spared the reforming zeal of Capability Brown and his imitators. Made between 1696 and 1725, it features allées with beech and hornbeam hedges, and three circular pools with fountains. This sober design is enlivened by urns, statuary and other ornaments of lead; the lawns are broken by clipped domes of evergreens and pairs of trees.

A garden of the same period that can still be seen is Levens Hall in Cumbria, made between 1690 and 1720. Its original topiary of yew and box, and its beech hedges, have now grown immense.

Inspired by the Jacobean period, topiary scenes can be found throughout the country, from the hare and hounds coursing along the top of a hedge to the peacock of countless cottage gardens and the abstract shapes of box corkscrews or yew pyramids.

Another seventeenth-century fashion, albeit short-lived, was the avenue, which would lead up to a great house. The trees were usually lime and English elm, or more rarely oak or sweet chestnut; later horse chestnut was also used.

With the rise of the Romantic movement, the charming old English gardens with their knots and pleached walks, arbours and topiary, went out of fashion. But many of the features were adapted to the cottage garden, in humbler form. And so with a new awareness of their special appeal, the makers of modern gardens often incorporate elements of ancient garden design.

O mistress mine! where are you roaming?
Oh! Stay and hear; your true love's coming,
That can sing both high and low.
Trip no further, pretty sweeting;
Journeys end in lovers meeting,
Every wise man's son doth know.

SHAKESPEARE *Twelfth Night*

The Secret Garden

My lovely garden too adjoining lies,
Of sweetest flowers, and of the richest dyes:
The tulip, jas'min, emony, and rose,
Of which we'll garlands for thy head compose.

PHILIP AYRES, 1638–1712

Secret gardens appeal to something that lies very deep in all of us. Perhaps, it is the sense of past romances, happy or tragic, that might have been acted out within those enclosing walls or hedges.

The luxury of a garden in which to sit and while away the hours was the privilege of noblemen and rich merchants in medieval times. These early gardens, illustrated in painted manuscripts, look charming, with their flowery meads and well-trained orchard trees, bordered perhaps by a trellised fence.

Sometimes a garden was created within a gar-den, increasing a sense of seclusion. These secret places, with their fountains, arbours and grassy walks were often planted with roses within the high hedges or walls that bounded them.

There was, at this time, no typically English style of garden: But while the Italians had their *giardino secreto* this was never the intimate enclosure that the English came to prefer, and which came to be incorporated into many manor-houses and mansion gardens in Tudor and Stuart times.

Secret gardens have no place in the great set piece landscapes, formal or informal. Beautiful as

these are in their way, all sense of intimacy has been lost. From the mid seventeenth century, the large gardens of manor houses and mansions had been expanded from partitioned designs to, first, undulating landscape, then into the consciously picturesque winding walks and shrubberies that Jane Austen's heroines would have known, and finally in Victorian times to the elaborate parterres of hothouse flowers.

But the cottage gardens never lost their hedges; and were the inspiration for the revival, in Edwardian times, of the hedged and walled garden. Gardens such as Hidcote and Sissinghurst are, in a sense, a series of secret, or at least intimately enclosed, gardens. So sure is their design that even when they are filled with visitors, the sense of romantic seclusion is strong. It has been said, even, that the whole of Hid-

cote is a secret garden, not intended to have anyone in it; it is a stillness in the midst of the open Cotswold hills, a work of art in which artistry never intrudes upon the magical atmosphere of the place.

The ideal secret garden today would be enclosed with a hedge or wall high enough to bar intruding eyes. It may lie, all unexpected, through a door in a wall that gives no clue to a garden beyond; or it may be a garden within a garden, screened from view by clipped yew or a hedge of eglantine, its entrance well away from the well-trodden paths.

In a secret garden the outside world is to be forgotten. It is unimportant whether, beyond the walls, there lies a noble landscape or the crowded streets of a town; the secret garden is wholly inward-looking. Within its bounds, a dream-like atmosphere permits the imagination to take wing.

Fragrance is an important component of the secret garden. No breezes disturb the sweetness of roses and honeysuckle, the almost tropical perfume of jasmine, the warm spice of wallflowers and carnations. Their perfume hangs suspended in the still air, arousing memories or a faint, sweet nostalgia.

The flowers in a secret garden are of soft, pale colours; it is a place of repose. Blush roses, pale honeysuckle, white jasmine, and wisteria of smoky blue are set off by dense, dark yew hedges or the muted terracotta of old walls. In the fresh spring grass, primroses and crocuses bloom with white

poet's narcissus and blue squills; the cherry blossom falls to mingle with these little blooms. Lily of the valley and lilacs follow, as the days draw out. In the summer borders, crystalline white lilies and pink phlox mix with creamy mock orange and the white fuzz of myrtle. The sun must reach into the little plot to warm the air; but there must be shade and shelter, too, for even in England, a summer's day can be hot until the sun goes down.

An idyllic secret garden can be created any-where. English town houses are often terraced into neat rows, with a simple railing in front; the garden is all behind, separated from its neighbour by a high wall. No-one can enter, except through the house; nothing could be more personal, more secluded. With walls topped by trellis, wreathed in clematis and vines and honeysuckle and the high-climbing roses with names such as 'Rambling Rector' or 'Bobbie James', privacy is ensured. Pots of sweet ger-anium, lemon verbena and bridal wreath, stood here

and there, give something of the feel of a Mediterranean courtyard garden.

Usually the larger cottage-style houses in English country towns are often built without regard for symmetry as a pantry is added here, a garden room there. This may create unexpected corners where, in the angle of two walls, a sunny, secret sitting place can be found, perhaps screened by a hedge or a barrier of flowering shrubs. Aromatic thyme and chamomile, growing in the cracks between paving stones, provide a fragrant carpet underfoot, the irregular tuffets in keeping with the charming in-and-outness of the cottage. The shelter of the cottage walls is an ideal place for the cherished myrtle, sprigs of which were traditionally carried in a bride's bouquet; passion flowers too thrive in the warmth of sturdy cob or stone walls. In days gone by many cottage gardens boasted a grape vine, its leaves providing a shady canopy in summer and the shelter of the walls helping the fruit to ripen. The sense of intimacy that forms the charm of a secret garden derives from its diminutive size. Thus it is that in the small gardens of today a secret garden may well have a place, providing a tranquil retreat from the bustle of modern life, or the setting for romance.

Arbours and Pavilions

The purpose of a pavilion is to be visited, rather than viewed. From its shelter, both owner and guests can survey the domain. In the garden at Westbury Court, Gloucestershire – virtually the only surviving formal garden in the Dutch style in England – the pavilions are set high above the walled garden, of canals and clipped hedges in which a worthy Dutch burger of the seventeenth century would have been entirely at ease. At Coleton Fishacre on the south

Devon coast, an open-sided gazebo built of stone and timber, half-concealed in vines and white wisteria, perches on the summit of a quarry, facing out to the dramatic vista of the sea and the Blackstone rocks. And in the garden at Great Dixter, old farm buildings have been transformed into loggias open to the lawns and borders.

Pavilions and garden houses vary from the classically elegant to the charmingly rustic — occasionally, even with a thatched roof to match the cottage or farmhouse they belong to. Often they are set about with flowers and decked with climbers; but the building, unless it is of the rudest construction, best concealed, is as important as the plants. These are buildings to use, not merely to admire.

In the typically English gardens that take their inspiration from more homely sources still — the idyllic cottage garden, especially — arbours are simpler structures, sometimes cut into the living yew, sometimes formed of a garland of roses or honeysuckle or jasmine on a rustic framework or a summerhouse. An arbour should be secluded, even secret, a place for a stolen kiss or an avowal of love, a refuge where letters can be read and re-read away from inquisitive eyes. It should afford shelter from sun and wind; and it should be set among fragrant flowers. A garden seat beneath an arch of yew, with a spray of roses or lilies nearby — so little as this can become an arbour.

The plants that grow on and about these simple garden structures are what, above all, them charm. In Italy, where the pergola originated, the luxuriant foliage of the vines gave shelter from the summer sun; in England, such protection is less often needed, but the charm of a walkway beneath sun-dappled foliage and fragrant flowers is undiminished. And the most romantic of these garden pathways will lead to a secluded seat or bower, garlanded like the pergola itself in flowers. At their feet wallflowers in spring, lilies in summer add their distinctive heady perfumes.

A garden should always be a place of rest, a refuge for the spirit; and in the words of the romantic poet Rupert Brooke, to entrap an English evening's magic hush.

*Summer
Idyll*

Fast fading violets cover'd
up in leaves;

And mid-May's eldest child,

The coming musk-rose,
full of dewy wine,

The murmurous haunt of
flies on summer eves.

KEATS

By Fountains and Streams

But still the Vine her ancient Ruby yields,
And still a Garden by the Water blows.

EDWARD FITZGERALD, from *The Rubaiyyat of Omar Khayyam*

Water in the garden has a special magic. Perhaps there is something deep in the human psyche which recalls the paradise gardens of Persia, in which water, in rills and fountains and pools, represented the life-giving quality of the oasis in a harsh, desert country.

Be that as it may, in garden after garden in England you will find water. It may be no more than

a simple well; or it may be an elaborate system of fountains, the creation of some wealthy potentate of an earlier century. In other gardens natural water is allowed to remain comparatively untamed, in streams and waterfalls and pools; though seldom will the weeds of the water's edge be allowed to remain. Instead, water-loving exotics such as the arum lily and the great yellow bog arum of North America yield, at the stream's edge, to Japanese candelabra primulas and feathery astilbes from China, to water iris with flowers like a clematis and the dramatic leaves of rodgersias.

In the large garden at Sheffield Park, a Capability Brown landscape to which have been added, with consummate skill, trees and shrubs from many lands, much of the beauty of the brilliant autumn colours lies in their contrast with dark conifers, the bright and the dark alike reflected in the wide lakes.

The sound of water is an important element in its appeal. The musical tinkle of water in a stone-lined rill descending over a series of small falls; the louder splash as it drops over a rocky chute; the repeated pattern of sound made by droplets falling from a fountain to a pool: these, with the other sounds of the garden, birdsong and the wind in the leaves, add another dimension to our enjoyment. In still water, reflections allow us yet another perception of the garden: the image of an overhanging branch, the mirrored delphiniums of the border, the calm echo of an arched bridge.

Romantic Vistas

A vista is not just a view; it is a view so contrived as to be seen in its most beautiful aspect, and specifically, one that is framed, by hedges, an avenue, mature trees, walls . . . In its original, seventeenth-century conception, it was associated with the idea of expansion into the surrounding country; the imagination takes wing, to create further distances. The typical eighteenth-century vista swept away its formal predecessor and led the eye through rolling landscape, planted with artistry, to a classical temple set in a grove of evergreens reflected in an expanse of water.

Today, a vista may also mean something less grandiose. It may be that the eye is drawn along a smooth grass path between high hedges towards a statue or urn. A paved path beneath pleached limes underplanted with spring flowers, as at Sissinghurst, is a more homely design that leads the eye to the unpretentious nutwalk. Clipped box hedges and a York stone path, in many a garden, suggest a stone seat where the hedges swell into a semi-circular enclosure, from which vantage point the vista can be enjoyed in reverse, back to a simple statue or a decorated lead urn planted with summer flowers.

Azaleas glowed with fierier red
To mark the spot where warriors bled
And still amid the ancient trees
In flaming brightness take the breeze,
But now in peace for those who seek
Of noble gardens soft they speak.

The classical landscape gardens were carefully planned so that at every turn the eye was guided to a fine prospect. One of the most beautiful in England, made by a banker, not by a professional landscape designer, is Stourhead. With its broad, still lakes, their sloping banks grassed or discreetly planted with rhododendrons, its fine trees, and its exquisite buildings of classical inspiration, it represents the idealized, idyllic landscape. The paths that wind along the lake shores were planned, in the eighteenth-century fashion, gradually to reveal ever-

changing vistas: the eye is drawn, now across the lake, past a simple arched bridge in the foreground, to the Pantheon; now to the Temple of Apollo on a height surrounded by trees. From each building, another can be seen as the focal point of a vista: the romantic Temple of Flora, the gothick Hermitage.

To see Stourhead as nearly as possible as it was conceived by its maker, Henry Hoare, visit it not at rhododendron time but when the dominant tones are the greens of grass and leaves and the grey of the skies reflected in the water. Then the magical ability of the

place to uplift the spirit is at its most pronounced, unmarred by the vivid rhododendron blooms that, despite their beauty, destroy some of the integrity of the design during their short season.

The gardens of this period in England are gardens of trees, grass, water, space and masonry; flowering plants were not used, and the rhododendrons at Stourhead are nineteenth-century additions. But the English love their flowers, and these classical gardens did not long satisfy them; the designer Humphrey Repton was the first to answer

the need, with gardens in which terraces and parterres linked the house to the park. The vistas over
rolling landscape that characterize the best English
country mansions were still there; but a style which
would develop into the more intimate gardens of
Edwardian times, a century later, was emerging.

The best Victorian gardens were formal without over-elaboration, as at Knightshayes Court in
Devon. From the long terrace the eye is drawn to a
simple circular pool and fountain in the lawn below
and, beyond it, through the landscaped park embel-

lished with magnificent trees, to the gentle, rolling
Devon country. At the end of the terrace, a wide circular lily pool, stone and grass bordered, is hidden
behind castellated yew hedges; only a simple statue
on a plinth decorates this peaceful enclosure, but the
statue draws the eye to the flowering trees on the
slope above.

In gardens such as Hidcote and Sissinghurst,
and a host of smaller gardens inspired by these two
great twentieth-century creations, the intimacy of
enclosed spaces was quite brilliantly combined

with the use of vistas so the sense of seclusion is never allowed to develop into claustrophobia. They look back to the manorial gardens with their lime walks, their pleached hornbeams, their alleys and avenues leading to embowered sitting places or to a statue set in an arch of yew.

At Hidcote the successive enclosures are set on either side of the main axis of the garden; they remain intimate, while the eye is free to range uninterrupted along the long axis bordered by clipped tapestry hedges, by pleached hornbeams on stilts, lifted by the upward incline of the land until finally the vista culminates in the enigmatic view of the open sky. The senses are bemused by the contrast between the intimacy, even secrecy, of the garden and the immensity of the heavens.

At Sissinghurst, too, the garden was planned around definite vistas. One of the most famous leads the eye from the White Garden, with its central, rose-smothered arch, through the Bishop's Gate and across the tower lawn to the massive yew hedges of the Rose Garden and its central rondel, leading the eye to a statue of a Bacchante.

Borrowed vistas, where a fine feature of the landscape seems by optical illusion to be part of the garden, are rarer in twentieth-century gardens. Few garden-makers today can say, as the owner of Castle Howard could just ten years ago, that he planned a new arboretum to extend 'as far as that hill', three miles away. Future generations will see the oaks and pines of Castle Howard in their glory, framing views of the magnificent Yorkshire countryside, as we today can enjoy the vistas of water, trees and rolling parkland of Capability Brown, and allow our imaginations to take wing as if we still lived in those spacious days.

The garden of a true cottager probably had few flowers in it; the space was needed to grow food for the large families of those days. So the image of a flowery patch where cabbages and peas jostled for room with pansies or wallflowers or hollyhocks, is a romanticized one. Distance lends charm to the fantasy image of the narrow path leading between fragrant herbs and primroses to the jasmine-wreathed porch, beloved by Victorian artists.

Many cottage garden plants date from long ago and can be found described in old herbals, of which the most famous is Gerard's, dating from 1597. Double flowers, filled with extra petals, are typical cottagers' plants. At first, there would have been the

The Cottage Garden

Soon will we have gold-dusted snapdragon,

Sweet-William with his homely cottage smell,

And stocks in fragrant blow

MATTHEW ARNOLD

JAMES MATTHEWS.

double forms of English wild flowers only: daisies, red and white; the double white primrose; double meadow cranesbill; double columbines, called Granny's bonnets; double lily of the valley and lady's smock. Curiously coloured forms of native flowers were valued too: violets in pink and sulphur as well as blue and white, primroses of 'lilac, burgundy, dingy and carmine'.

Other plants were valued for their utility: prunella or self-heal for treating wounds and sores; meadowsweet, sweet flag and other strewing herbs for muting unpleasant odours; horehound for coughs; feverfew for headaches and fever. Later these were joined by plants from beyond England's shores.

Even as early as the sixteenth century, English gardens

were being enriched by introductions from other countries, at first from the Mediterranean lands and later from America, then Japan and China, South Africa and the Antipodes. Some of these early introductions, too, are cherished cottage garden plants, especially those that were useful as well as beautiful. The roots of iris were used in *pot-pourri*; the crimson petals of *Rosa gallica*, the apothecary's rose, were used to make fragrant rose water.

A characteristic of the true cottage garden of the past is that it showed evidence, not of wealth but of skill and devoted care. Even the annuals and biennials with their homely English names were

E.A.CHADWICK

grown, more often than not, from seed saved or exchanged with a neighbour rather than bought: love-in-a-mist and sweet sultan, cornflowers and snapdragons, hollyhocks and Canterbury bells, sweet Williams, candytuft, forget-me-nots and lark-spur. The fragrant old laced and clove pinks would be passed from one garden to another by means of slips; roses were grown from cuttings or suckers; the old double red peony, and its rarer white and blush counterparts, from divisions; crown imperials in tawny orange and yellow, from their pungently

foxy bulbs. Roots of creeping thyme and the pungent little Corsican mint, of pennyroyal and marjoram, were exchanged between neighbours and set between the flagstones or crazy paving, or at the edge of the brick paths, that led from the gate to the honeysuckle-wreathed porch.

Often, a low wall surrounds the little plot. All manner of flowers seed themselves in the crumbling mortar: wallflowers and snapdragons, golden alyssum and valerian in pink, red and white. Houseleeks are set there, and the silvery-white snow-in-sum-

mer. In the shadier nooks little ferns – rustyback or ric-rac fern, wall rue, and dwarf maidenhair – make themselves at home with the yellow fumitory. Where a hedge replaced the wall, it was often embellished with honeysuckle or the wild musk rose. The hedge itself might be of sweet brier, the wild rose.

In such small plots, little plants were treasured: auriculas with simple names – Old Dusty Miller, Old Irish Blue – the Hen and Chickens daisy, gold-laced polyanthus, the double crimson wallflower called Old Bloody Warrior, and the double sticky

Nellie or catchfly. Double snowdrops pierce the cold earth in midwinter; soon after, the double daffodil Van Sion flaunts its bright, ragged blooms.

The names of flowers are often a guide to their antiquity and standing; cottage gardeners rarely learned the botanical epithets, and their love of their plants is revealed in the English names they bestowed on them. Bachelor's buttons, periwinkle, cowslip, marigold, Maltese cross, thrift, campion, heart's ease, pasque flower, sweet cicely: these are all plants of the true cottage garden.

The Rose Garden

The rose is, more than any other, the flower of romance. The combination of beauty and fragrance acts irresistibly upon our sentiments to weave a spell to which countless rose gardens large and small, the length and breadth of England, testify.

Of all the roses grown, it is the old shrub roses and their rambling counterparts that speak most eloquently of romance. Their very names are redolent of times past. The York and Lancaster rose, its parti-coloured flowers of white, carnation and rose madder recalls the Wars of the Roses in fifteenth-century England; and 'Tuscany', the name now borne by the rich crimson Old Velvet Rose, is described in Gerard's *Herbal* of 1597. The striped 'Rosa Mundi' is of less certain

date; but an enduring tradition links it with Henry II's Fair Rosamond, who died in 1176.

Different groups of the oldest roses also have evocative names: the damask roses, the Provence or cabbage roses beloved of painters, and the alba roses, where the white rose of York belongs. The moss rose, which earns its name from the aromatic, mossy coat of green or brown that covers the calyx and stem of the flower, appeared during the eighteenth century. It has been cherished ever since as much for its cottagey charm and its fragrance (which comes both from the petals and from the 'moss') as for its range of colour from white through pink to deepest midnight

crimson. The common pink moss has been immortalized in the porcelain of the Worcester factory, in the pattern known as 'Blind Earl': for the rosebuds that decorate the borders of plates and dishes and saucers are raised in high relief, so that the sightless Earl of Coventry could still enjoy his beloved roses.

In gardens, these old roses are allowed to grow into informal bushes, their fresh green or grey-jade leaves studded in summer with bouquets of perfumed petals. Still more generous are the climbing and rambling roses, which fill old orchard trees or garland arbours and bowers, pergolas and trellis screens. The extreme formality of French rose gardens, each bush or climber trained to a precise geometric shape, has never appealed to the English, with their love of the informal, the relaxed. Cascades of perfumed ramblers tumbling from ancient yews, their creamy blossoms whitened by contrast with the gardens, it is in design. Roses look well in a setting of paving and masonry, or among clipped yew hedges; and many English gardens excel in both. In simpler surroundings, a wooden post and rail fence around a cottage garden is often clad in fragrant

dark foliage; perfumed swags of blooms wreathing ropes that link a progression of pillars; a rustic porch half-concealed beneath fragrant petals: these are more in tune with the English taste.

Where there is formality in English rose rambling roses such as the apple-scented 'Albéric Barbier' or tawny pink 'Albertine'. A simple summerhouse may be transformed by its cloak of roses; an arch of roses marks the transition from one enclosed garden to another; a tripod of poles in a

95

border supports a pyramid of roses among the humbler flowers of summer.

France was the country where most varieties were raised, but England is the land of the roses of York and Lancaster, the white and the red, and of the heraldic Tudor rose; and she has made the roses of France and of China, the attar roses of Kazanlik, and the Persian yellow rose, her own as well.

And wholly English are the hybrid musk roses, bred by the Rev. Joseph Pemberton, in his vicarage garden at Havering-atte-Bower. These vigorous, perpetual-flowering shrub roses inherit from their distant musk rose ancestor the precious quality of a rich free-floating perfume. Of them Vita Sackville-West, who treasured so many roses at Sissinghurst, wrote in her poem *The Garden:*

> . . . Rose of the World; th'embroidered Tuscany;
> The scented Cabbage, and the Damascene;
> Sweet Briar, lovelier named the eglantine'
> But above all the Musk
> With classic names, Thisbe, Penelope,
> Whose nectarous load grows heavier with the dusk
> And like a grape too sweetly muscadine.

With their great burst of flower at midsummer and second flush of huge swags in autumn, the hybrid musk roses have added immeasurably to the pleasures of the English flower border.

In an English Orchard

Beneath these fruit-tree boughs that shed

Their snow-white blossoms on my head,

With brightest sunshine around me spread

Of spring's unclouded weather,

In this sequestered nook how sweet

To sit upon my orchard seat.

WORDSWORTH *The Green linnet*

The Fragrant Garden

Romantic gardens appeal to all our five senses, but often, a fragrance or aroma will prove the most evocative. There is a special joy in seeking out fragrance, perhaps a richly perfumed crimson rose, or picking a posy of lily of the valley in spring or clove-scented pinks in summer.

The very colours of fragrant flowers are the tender colours of romance: white, blush and rose, crimson and violet and primrose yellow. It is rare to find a vivid flower with much scent: they have no need of it, for they flaunt themselves in other ways. And it happens that these gentle colours are the very tones that best show up at dusk, when fragrance is at its sweetest. The pale globes of white roses, the ghostly blooms of mock orange, the crystalline trumpets of

the Madonna lily, gleam in the fading light long after the brighter flowers have been eclipsed by night.

The dying embers of the day work a different magic on the crimsons and purples and the candy-pinks of so many scented roses. These hold the fading light for a brief moment glowing with incandescence, before leaving the stage to the ice-pale tones. At dusk, too, the special quality of night-scented plants is revealed; for as they recede into the darkness, their perfume comes floating on the air to greet us. Tobacco flowers, modestly folded into pleated khaki by day, expand into flared white trumpets exhaling sweetness by night. The dowdy little night-scented stock, not worth a second glance by day even could you see its colourless flowers, fills the

air with its warm, clove-and-almond perfume. And honeysuckle and jasmine, indispensable in the fragrant garden, redouble their efforts by night.

There are also the plants with aromatic foliage that need the gentle touch of a passing hand, or even of a careless skirt, to release their resinous pungence into the air. Lavender – who has not run a hand, absently, along a spike of purple lavender and inhaled its curiously old-fashioned fragrance, the turpentine Russian sage, soft-textured lad's love with its strange, sharp aroma; these are plants to caress, to pluck and crush between finger and thumb. Thyme, which hugs the ground, gives off its herby fragrance when scuffed by passing feet; and chamomile is used to make the fragrant lawns of old English gardens in

'And because the breath of flowers is far sweeter in the air (where it comes and goes like the warbling of music) than in the hand, therefore nothing is more fit for that delight than to know what be the flowers and plants that do best perfume the air.'

FRANCIS BACON

place of grass, so every step releases into the air its powerful aroma of apples.

The Mediterranean myrtle, which thrives in warm corners in English gardens, is held in special affection. Brides like to carry a sprig of myrtle, dark of leaf and creamy-white of fragrant flower, in their bouquets. The ceremony over, the precious sprig is rooted, and the new little plant is set against a warm wall to remind the couple, as it grows, of their courtship and their wedding day.

Perhaps the special quality of fragrance is its ability to heighten our emotions, to intensify our moods. Where scented flowers and leaves are set with skill — in bowers and arbours, in walled gardens and on sun-trapping terraces, in cool walks where pale flowers gleam and by fountains where the air sparkles with droplets — the impressions we take away of that garden will be transmuted into an enduring memory, reawakened at unexpected moments to come by an echo of the same fragrance.

Framed by Roses

There are few more seductive pleasures in life than walking into a room filled with the heady scent of roses. The sweet-smelling gardens of summer can be transported inside by framing windows and doors with wreaths of tangled rosebuds, whose

scent will waft through on the evening air. French windows, thrown open over a balcony whose balustrades are intertwined with roses in a myriad shades of pale pink or soft butter yellow, conjures a scene as romantic as that from Shakespeare's *Romeo and Juliet*. Rambling roses mingled with honeysuckle or jasmine or the heavy blue and white flower tresses of wisteria make for a truly intoxicating combination.

The wild briar rose, its branches furled in a haphazard arrangement about a country cottage door, epitomizes a truly English vision of the rural garden. The heavy blossoms of the damask rose, trailed across a portico, characterize the English country house, a

theme continued inside with roses strewn across deep, chintz-covered sofas and swagged curtains.

Whether trained with trellis, grown in Versailles tubs on a patio or allowed to tumble in abandoned profusion, roses around windows or doors will soften grey stone or red brickwork in summer and add colour in autumn with a harvest of scarlet hips.

Roses of different hue create delightful colour combinations; variant shades of the same colour, too – tones of clotted cream and yellow; crushed-strawberry pink with paler shades; tones of apricot; or as a real tour de force, all-white roses to be viewed on a moonlit night – a feast for the senses.

A Woodland Muse

Where'er you walk cool gales shall
fan the glade;

Trees, where you sit, shall crowd into
a shade;

Where'er you tread, the blushing
flow'rs shall rise,

And all things flourish where you
turn your eyes.

POPE *Pastorals*

❧ *Index* ❧

Numbers in bold indicate illustrations

Acknowledgements

The publishers wish to thank the following for permission to reproduce the illustrations: Didier Aaron Inc., New York p 54. Clive Boursnell* pp 24–5. Boys Syndication pp 47, 57; pp 92–3 and 94 left photos by Jacqui Hurst. Bridgeman Art Library, London with acknowledgements to: Victoria and Albert Museum, London pp 8–9, 93 (inset), 98 (inset); Chris Beetles Ltd., London pp 32, 96; Private Collection pp 48–9; The British Library Board p 53 right; Bonham's London pp 66, 75; The Lindley Library, Royal Horticultural Society, London p 69 (inset); Christopher Wood Gallery, London pp 71 (inset), 78, 80; Harris Museum and Art Gallery, Preston, Lancs p 100; Warrington Museum and Art Gallery p 109. Linda Burgess/Insight pp 28–9, 53 left, 78–9, 82, 87, 98–99, 110 left, 111 below left, 112–3. Christie's, London p 107. Fine Art Photographic Library, London pp 44 (inset), 85, 86, 113 (inset). Garden Picture Library, London p 16 photo Stephen Robson; pp 20 and 109 left photos Gary Rogers; pp 67 and 76 photos Marianne Majerus; p 106 right photo Steven Wooster; p 110 above right photo Marijke Heuff; p 110 below right photo Clive Boursnell. John Glover pp 14, 44–5, 60, 108 left. Mick Hales p 97. Jerry Harpur pp 6–7, 25, 50, 72–3, 81, 83, 104–5. Andrew Lawson pp 22 (inset), 24 (inset), 62, 64–5, 91. Manchester City Art Gallery p 61. S & O Mathews pp 22–3, 70, 74, 84, 89 (inset), 94 right, 102, 103 left, 111 above left and right. Tania Midgley pp 30–31, 33, 40, 42, 43, 106 above left. John Miller* pp 34–5, 36–7, 38–9. The National Trust Photographic Library pp 26; pp 27 and 41 photos John Bethell. Norfolk Country Library p 95. Clay Perry* pp 19, 49 (inset), 52, 56, 58–59, 63, 68–9, 90, 100–101. Walter Pfeiffer pp 10–11, 13, 18, 55, 103 right. The Royal Horticultural Society, Lindley Library pp 12, 17. Victoria and Albert Museum, London pp 84–91 (borders). Photographs by courtesy of Christopher Wood Gallery, London/Private Collections pp 28 (inset), 77, 88–89, 106 below left. George Wright* p 46.

*©George Weidenfeld and Nicholson Ltd.

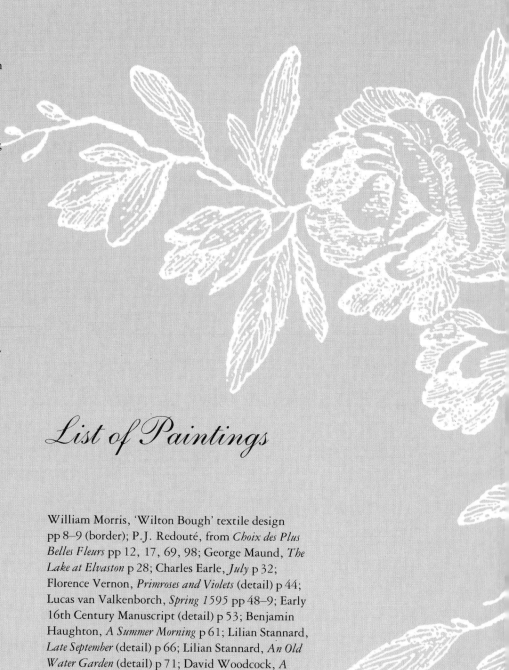

List of Paintings